To Lora
Christmas 1981

With Love,
Mom

Before and Ever After

Love Poems
by Ed Cunningham
Illustrated by
David R. Miles

Hallmark Crown Editions

Before and Ever After

A Banquet of Spring

Basketless
  and blanketless,
we dined
  on the look of that park,
finding lilacs
  and willows
delicious to behold,
  skies for the drinking
and roses,
  a dessert for the eyes.
Watching together
  we settled close
and let the morning
  become our picnic.

Worst Party I Ever Went to

Ate burnt hamburgers,
greeted frozen people,
heard re-cycled jokes
followed by polluted laughs,
drank 3.1 cans
of 3.2 beer,
met you,
danced a few slow ones,
got off in a corner,
learned all about you,
told all about me,
and drove us home
for the very first time...

Best party I ever went to.

One Enchanted Evening

There we were
very far off Broadway
belting out
our first show stopper
me
a little flat on my Rogers
'you
a little hazy on your Hammerstein
but somehow we clicked
became
stars together
and our encores
filled all the silences
of that big empty house.

A Vanishing Act

Let me show you
a different sort of magic
first
we lower the lights
almost to darkness
then
we spin this ancient disc
close our eyes
and half-listen
to the small Italian
with the large voice
sing of lost loves
while I hold you in my arms
like so
and we slide
back and forth
round and round
slowly
slowly
until the time
the room, the music
and the dance
have disappeared—
and only we remain.

The Ex-3rd Stringer

As the ball is snapped
I throw a fake block
    at a blitzing typewriter salesman,
slant left
    between a pair
        of wheezing bartenders
buttonhook
    and grab a wobbly pass
        from an even wobblier C.P.A.,
sidestep
    a fifty-year-old priest
        and a rotund English instructor
and gallop twelve yards
    for a T.D.
        and a victorious hug
from my
    own personal
        and very sexy cheerleader.

On the Town

Caught live
in a place we wouldn't be
caught dead
we made the best of things
reading amateur erotica
carved and scribbled
across our table
complimenting short-order cuisine
served by professional zombies
tapping our toes
to noises piped in from some zoo
laughing
sparkling
enjoying each other as seldom before
toasting
to never having to be
in a place like that
alone.

20th Century Rendezvous

We didn't exactly race
slow motion
through fields of waving wildflowers
in soft focus
and evaporate
into a lyrical kiss,
but somehow
in the middle of a crowded terminal
despite two leaden Samsonites
and four weary feet
we struggled together
and were
god so glad
to see each other.

Art Appreciation I

After five jealous minutes
of watching you
watch Vincent van Gogh
I feel a biting suspicion
that you and he
share delicious secrets
forever hidden from my eyes,
and a growing realization
that I am being
upstaged
by an Old Master.

An Accidental Valentine

Noticing the note on your desk top
    that began, "Dear Mom and Dad"
and was plainly none of my business,
    I carefully devoured every syllable...
discovered
    certain rave notices about myself
too flattering to repeat
    and hoped
your folks would enjoy hearing from you
    as much as I had.

Sunday Afternoon

Look…
it's June outside
and I'll bet I know
where we can find a slow boat
and a whole lake full of time
to lie back and dream
of a world
without Mondays.

Far Into Summer

On
that beach
where time with you
was love
we kissed the day to sleep
and spoke
of all our lives
as
night happened
slowly above us
filling our sea with stars.

Since It's Prime Time

Why don't we
stage a love scene
live and in color
right here
in front of our t.v. set
and let all these
comic secretaries
grim U.S. marshals
and rugged private eyes
watch *us*
for a change?

There in Fun-Land Park

Met a kid today
I'd never known before
running and laughing her way
through acres of crazy contraptions
designed to make grown-ups
feel dizzy or silly or scared,
a delightful little girl…
the one
you must have been.

And Now, Ladies and Gentlemen...

Did you hear the one about the guy
who had this sort of uncontrollable
urge to be, ah...shall we say...
uncommitted. So he meets up with
this gal, see, and she's the
same way, if you know what I mean,
and well, to make a long story short,
they begin to kind of dig each other
and...are you ready for this?...
they start getting serious
and...guess what?...before you know it,
they fall in love and mess up
what could have turned out
to be a really good joke.

Across the Board

Shrewdly, patiently
we duel...
Master Strategist
vs.
Seasoned Gambler...
while the hours wind themselves
around the table
till we're closer in our silence
than we were the time before...
and though we take turns being winner
no one's
really ever lost...

not in our game.

At the Cocktail Party

We were great tonight
Formidable Allies
in the Never-Ending Struggle
for Human Rights
Eloquent Crusaders
against the forces
of Prejudice, Hypocrisy and Chauvinism,
hacking our way
through rooms full of Barbarians,
but
now that the battle is over,
I'm beginning to think
how fine you'd look
outside
that suit of armor.

Lifestyle

As we listen
    to this beautiful couple
tell of life
    in their fun complex
of wearing swimsuits
    all day Saturday
and hiring live-in
    social directors,
of blending
    devastating daiquiris
and throwing
    weekend-long parties,
of keeping so busy
    being beautiful
they've never had time
    to be lonely,
I only want to squeeze your hand
    and whisper
how delighted I am
    to be on the outside
looking in
    with you.

Your Instant Cowboy

Something about
　　the way you watched me
clumping
　　down the bridle path
on my guaranteed
　　gentle-as-they-come
mare
　　made me
sit a little taller
　　in the old saddle
grin precariously
　　and wish
for the first time
　　since I was eleven
that I were John Wayne.

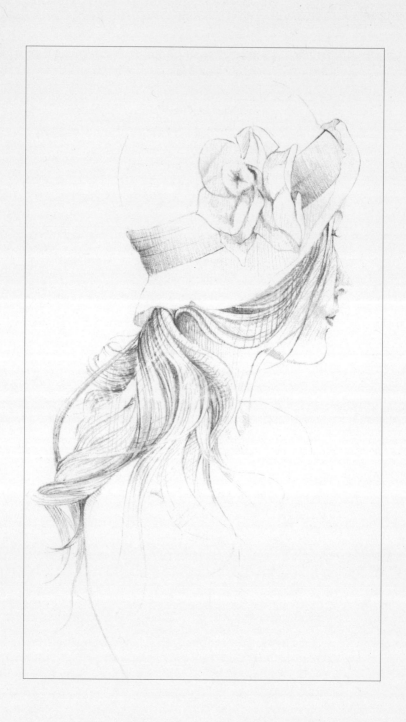

Keep the Faith

Please hang on
to whatever it is that helps you be
who you are and how you are
and still lets you see
who I am and where I am.
Whether or not it's
that old-time religion,
it's plenty good enough for me.

After Office Hours

Nasty of scowl
hyper of tension
one
minor factor from a major factory
lurches home in a state
of teeth-grinding hack
to be welcomed by
the one,
the only—
MISS INFORMALITY OF CHESTNUT CIRCLE
she of the unstarched hugs and
untimed kisses she of the unprogrammed
winks and unscheduled wisecracks she
who alone can conjure in me that
hang-loose-school's-out-Saturday
kind of feeling
that lasts
till
bedtime.

That Just-Right Gift

I was
Macy-ed, Penney-ed, Sears-ed,
notioned, baubled, keepsaked, trinketed,
boutiqued and head-shopped out
by the time
I settled on the little item
You are about to unwrap.
It is, of course,
just what every young girl needs:
a tiny gold piano
that plays something longhair
and sort of pretty
whenever you lift the lid.
I won't be hurt
if you laugh a bit
when you see what it is
oh,
but please love this…
I need you to.

The Necessities

All my life ever needed
   was its coupla drinks
      its coupla laughs
     its little song-and-dance
      on Friday night...
Those well-rehearsed routines
   I thought such fun.
All my life ever needed
   was its halfway highs
      its not-too lows
     its cozy little company
      of friends...
that party-candle glow
   I thought so warm.
All my life ever needed
   was its sack-out space
      its work-out place
     its means of getting smoothly
      back and forth...
that painless pointless trip
   I thought was living
back in the good ol'
   click-on, click-off days
   before I learned
All my life ever needed
   was you.

Soliloquy at Intermission

Show me a dame
who'd pass up her big night
at the Philharmonic
just to sit in this dump
watching beat-up Bogie flicks
with a mug like me
and I'll show you a dame with class.
Real class.

Here's lookin' at you, kid.

An Autumn Spectacular

Overhead
a short-circuited sky
crackled and flamed
in all directions
Below
a night-time city
blinked and blazed itself
through the streaming windshield
while we
engrossed in more beautiful matters
hardly noticed the light show
being held in our honor.

Hearthside

All
of the world
that interests me
shines here in this room
when your eyes
catch the dancing
your hands
hold the warmth
your smile
becomes part
of the fire.

A Sober Reflection

This was the birthday
by which I'd planned to be
wise
well-defined
living in a movie set
driving a precision machine
dressing like a talk-show host
with my pockets full of negotiable blessings
and a little salted away.
Needless to say
what happened was
none of the above…
so bless you
for not expecting
my Happy-Birthday-Boy routine
and for all those candles
you thoughtfully failed
to ignite.

Towards Morning

During
those hours
between 4:00 a.m.
and five minutes later
I began to think my apartment
was the capital of loneliness
and that nothing would do
but the sound
of your sleepy voice
so I dialed
and though you probably have
no idea
what we talked about
maybe you'll remember
watching
the sunrise
person-to-person.

Before and Ever After

I remember a January
    with someone who liked Baudelaire
    and hot spiced wine,
Yes, and a July with someone else
    whose dearest pleasures were
        drive-in movies and ice cold beer,
Then, let's see, there was an April
    when I played
        The Sensuous Tennis Instructor,
Not to mention, a September
    when someone kept me dancing
        to the cast album of Hair,
But most of all,
    I remember wishing
        there were someone
        who could fill
    all the seasons of my life
    with love,
And when you finally arrived
    believe me
        I was ready.

The Couple in the Photo

They seem so unposed,
so easy in their love.
Note:
his protective arm,
her contented smile.
It's as though they couldn't imagine
being anywhere but
together.
Beautiful, don't you think,
that after all this time
those two happy people
are still
us.

In Our Winter Studio

Two passionate sculptors
we worked slowly
between kisses
and
detail-by-detail
a personality emerged
who was
by the American flag in his right hand
a patriot
by the burgundy bottle in his left
a bon vivant
by the splendor of his cap and scarf
a fashion plate
by the way he smiled up at the sun
an optimist
then
we shivered back indoors
to celebrate success
pleased and proud
to have left upon that snowscape
a twenty-four hour
masterpiece.

A Dedication

In dawn's wakening smile,
   in bright new promises of morning,
     I have seen your eyes…
In music of mid-day,
   in sweet soaring vibrancy of earthsongs,
     I have heard your voice…
In evening's warm caress,
   in sheltering closeness of sunset,
     I have felt your touch…
All things beautiful in my world
   have breathed the magic,
     the mystery, the miracle of you…
I have loved you this day.

This book was designed and illustrated by David R. Miles.
The typeface is Romanee, designed by Jan van Krimpen
to accompany the only surviving italic of the seventeenth
century Amsterdam founder Cristoffel Van Dijck.
Printed on Hallmark Buff Vellux Paper.
The cover is bound with book cloth and Torino paper.